# Being a Good Citizen

## A KIDS' GUIDE TO COMMUNITY INVOLVEMENT

by Rachelle Kreisman
with illustrations by Tim Haggerty

RED
CHAIR
·PRESS·

Please visit our website at **www.redchairpress.com** for more high-quality products for young readers.

**Publisher's Cataloging-In-Publication Data**
(Prepared by The Donohue Group, Inc.)

Kreisman, Rachelle.
 Being a good citizen : a kids' guide to community involvement / by Rachelle Kreisman ; with illustrations by Tim Haggerty. -- [First edition].

 pages : illustrations ; cm. -- (Start smart: community)

 Summary: Whether it's raising money for a charity, spending time with a senior citizen, or cleaning up a park, getting involved in your community is a great way to help others and feel good about yourself. Includes fun facts.
 Interest age level: 006-009.
 Edition statement supplied by publisher.
 Includes index.
 Issued also as an ebook.
 ISBN: 978-1-939656-95-7 (library hardcover)
 ISBN: 978-1-939656-96-4 (paperback)

 1. Community life--Juvenile literature.  2. Public officers--Juvenile literature.  3. Social service--Juvenile literature.  4. Voluntarism--Juvenile literature.  5. Community life.  6. Public officers.  7. Social service.  8. Voluntarism.  I. Haggerty, Tim.  II. Title.

HM761 .K744 2015
307                                                           2014957487

**Illustration credits:** p. 1, 5, 6, 10, 12, 14, 16, 18, 20,, 22, 24, 25, 27, 31, 32: Tim Haggerty

**Photo credits:** Cover, p.1, 4, 8 (top inset), 11 (large), 13, 20, 21 (bottom): iStock; p. 5, 6, 7, 8 (top large), 8 (bottom), 9, 10, 11 (small top left), 11 (small middle left), 12, 14, 15, 16, 17, 18, 19, 21 (top), 23, 24, 25 , 26, 27: Shutterstock; p. 32: Courtesy of the author, Rachelle Kreisman

This series first published by:
Red Chair Press LLC          PO Box 333          South Egremont, MA 01258-0333

Printed in the United States of America

032017 3P WRZF15

# Table of Contents

Words in **bold type** are defined in the glossary.

# CHAPTER 1

# Community Living

Everyone is part of a **community**. A community is a place where people live, work, and play. Each community is made up of neighborhoods. Those neighborhoods are made up of people. You are one of those people! So you are part of a community.

Good **citizens** make the community a better place. A citizen is a person who lives in a certain place. It can be a town or city, state, or country.

How can you be a good citizen? Make a difference in your community! Learn about your elected officials and follow rules. Get involved in community activities. Be a good neighbor and help others. Do you want to learn more? Of course, you do! Keep reading to find out more about how you can be a good citizen.

# CHAPTER 2

# Elected Officials

**T**he United States has elected officials. Citizens vote them into office. Elected officials make rules called **laws**. They also make decisions about **taxes** and how government money should be spent.

The country has a national government. It makes laws that say how the United States should be run. The president is the leader of the country.

## FUN FACT

The capital of the United States is Washington, D.C. It is named after George Washington, the first U.S. president. Washington, D.C. is a district that is not part of a state. The D.C. stands for District of Columbia.

Washington, D.C.

Americans choose officials by voting.

In 2014, Mayor Bill DeBlasio of New York City marches in a parade.

Each state has its own government too. The states follow national laws and have their own state laws. A **governor** is the leader of a state.

States are made up of counties. Almost every state has county governments. The title of the county leader varies by state.

States also have city governments. Each city has a leader called a **mayor**. The mayor oversees fire and police departments, schools, and **public transportation**.

The mayor works with the city **council**. It is a group of people who make the laws for the city. They are elected by the citizens. The council has meetings to talk about local issues. Members work together to solve problems and to decide how city money should be spent.

Council meetings are usually open to the public. Anyone is welcome to attend and voice their opinions.

## DID YOU KNOW?

A city hall is the building of the city government. It is where the mayor's office is located. It is also where the city council usually holds its meetings.

City Hall, Houston, TX

Towns have their own local governments too. Elected officials work to make decisions for the town.

States also have school districts. Each district is made up of the public schools in the area. A **school board** is a group of people elected by local citizens to run each district. Board members make decisions for the public school system. They work to give students the best possible education.

School boards often meet monthly. Most meetings are open to the public.

🏠 Most school board meetings are open to the public.

# CHAPTER 3

# Get Involved

**G**ood citizens are involved in the community. They get to know their neighbors and other citizens They work to make their community a better place to live.

What can you do to get involved? Start by taking part in after-school activities. Join a community center or youth group. They have programs and activities just for kids. You can have fun and make new friends.

**JUST JOKING!**

**Q:** Did you hear the joke about the community center's roof?

**A:** Never mind—it's over your head!

COMMUNITY CENTER

⌂ After-school activities can be a good way to try new things.

Another way to get involved is to follow local news. That will let you know what is going on in your community. For example, you might learn that your police department is teaching a free bike safety class. Maybe you will want to take the class.

How can you follow the news? Read school and local newspapers. Watch the local news with a parent. Then talk about what you learned. Ask family members their opinions and share your own.

Being a good citizen includes voting. Citizens can vote in local, state, and national elections. You must be 18 years old to vote in most states.

Every four years, citizens elect the president of the United States. Kids can vote too! How? Many schools invite kids to take part in a **mock election**. It helps students learn about the election process.

## DID YOU KNOW?

People in the United States vote on Election Day. It is always the Tuesday after the first Monday in November.

VOTE    VOTE    BALLOTS

How else can you get involved? Learn about your community history. Visit museums and town **landmarks**. Go with a parent to take a tour of your city hall. Meet some of your elected officials. Attend a school board meeting.

Some schools have a student council. They organize special activities and help make school decisions. If you have a student council, you can vote to elect officers. You may also want to serve on the council!

🏠 Most museums welcome students.

# CHAPTER 4

# Be a Role Model

Do you have a **role model**? A role model is a person who sets a good example. He or she inspires others. Good role models are good citizens.

You can be a role model too! Start by being a good friend and family member. Be kind, friendly, and polite. Saying "please" and "thank you" goes a long way. And don't forget to smile! It can make you feel happier. Your smile can make others happier too.

## TRY THIS!

Practice smiling. Do you feel happier? If not, smile often throughout the day. It should make you feel better. Try sharing your smile with others. Count how many people smile back.

A good citizen respects others. How can you show your respect? Treat others the way you would want to be treated. Stick up for someone who is not being treated with respect.

Good citizens also respect **property**. They take good care of other people's things. That includes community property. For example, when you go to the park, keep it clean. If you borrow a library book, treat it with care.

**JUST JOKING!**

**Q:** Why did the student stop using her pencil?

**A:** She didn't see the point of it!

Good citizens follow rules and laws. You may not like every rule or law, but they were made for a reason. Rules and laws help keep order. They also help keep people safe.

Families have home rules. One rule may be to have good manners. Another rule may be to keep your room clean. Many families also have rules about safety. What rules do you have at home?

Schools have rules for students to follow. "Listen to the teacher" and "be kind to others" are two school rules. They keep kids safe and help them learn.

Communities have laws to keep citizens safe. For example, drivers must follow speed limits to stay safe on the road. Some laws keep communities clean. If someone litters, that person may have to pay a fine.

# CHAPTER 5

# Help Others

Good citizens are active in community service. They volunteer their time to help others. They also donate items and money to people in need. That can make a big difference in people's lives.

Helping others can make a difference in your life too. It can bring you a lot of joy! Doing good deeds can inspire others to do the same.

## FUN FACT

Doing a kind act can make you just as happy as receiving one. Both affect your brain in the same way. They make your brain give off feel-good chemicals, say scientists.

What can you do to help others? Start by doing random acts of kindness. Those acts are small, kind gestures. For example, draw a picture for a friend or family member. Say a friendly "hello" to a neighbor. Give flowers to a teacher. Hold the door open for the next person. Read a book to a younger child. Give someone a compliment.

You can do random acts of kindness every day. See how many kind acts you can do for others.

Are you looking for other ways to help? You have come to the right place! Choose a **charity** you want to help. Save some of your money to donate.

You can also donate things. Give away old clothes, shoes, and toys that are in good shape. Kids in need will be happy that you did!

Donate food to a local food bank. They give food to people in need. Check first to find out what foods they accept. Then organize a neighborhood food drive.

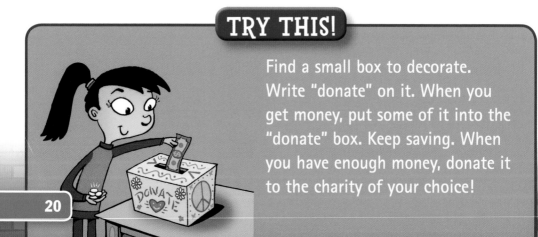

## TRY THIS!

Find a small box to decorate. Write "donate" on it. When you get money, put some of it into the "donate" box. Keep saving. When you have enough money, donate it to the charity of your choice!

Volunteer your time to help your community! Start close to home. Help a parent with the laundry or the dishes. Rake leaves or shovel snow for a neighbor.

If you like animals, help out at a local animal shelter. Volunteer with your family at a soup kitchen. You can help make and serve meals for people in need. Visit an assisted living home to bring some cheer. If you play music or sing, put on a recital. You can also make and give out greeting cards cards at a nursing home or hospital.

# CHAPTER 6

# Protect Earth

Good citizens take care of Earth. You can help too! Start by keeping your community clean. Get friends and family to clean up litter from parks and beaches. Animals can choke on litter if they mistake it for food.

Cut down on your use of electricity. Most electricity is made when fuel is burned. That **pollutes** the air. Turn off lights when you don't need them. Use less heat when it is cold outside. Instead, dress in warmer clothes.

## DID YOU KNOW?

Ask a parent if you can plant a tree. Trees help clean the air. They remove harmful gas from the air and give off oxygen. Oxygen is a gas that people and animals can't live without.

You can also help Earth if you follow the three R's. The first R is **reduce**. It means you should make less trash. If you buy items with less packaging, you will have less to throw away. Better yet, see if you can borrow something instead of buying it.

Help keep plastic bags from becoming trash. The bags can blow away and end up in trees, parks, rivers, and oceans. There, the bags can harm animals. If you buy something, say "no, thanks!" to plastic bags. Instead, bring reusable cloth bags when you shop.

The next R is **reuse**. It means "to use again." When you donate your old toys and clothes, they can be reused.

If you own books that you no longer read, donate them to a school or charity. That way, your books can be used again.

Save the wrapping paper from gifts you opened. Use the paper again when you need to wrap a gift. Writing a report? Use both sides of the paper.

## FUN FACT

Trash is a growing problem. The average American throws out 4 ½ pounds a day. What does that add up to each year? About 1,600 pounds of trash per person! (That's about the same weight as 100 bowling balls!)

Do you know the last R? It stands for **recycle**. Materials that are recycled are made into something new. Many communities have recycling programs. People often put items to be recycled in a bin. They leave the bin by the curb for pick-up. People can also take items to a recycling center.

Items that can be recycled include paper, cardboard, cans, glass bottles, and plastics. Before you recycle something, see if you can reuse it instead.

JUST JOKING!

**Q:** What did the eraser say to the paper?

**A:** Nothing. It just drew a blank!

# CHAPTER 7

# Get Started

Being a good citizen helps make your community a better place. It also makes you feel good about yourself. Are you ready? Then get involved in your community! Join an after-school club. Visit your city hall. Donate your old toys and clothes to other kids in need. Clean up litter in a park. Spend time with an older person who lives at an assisted living home. The list goes on and on.

Don't forget—good citizens are also good role models. Follow rules at home, in school, and in your community. Show off your good manners. Respect other people and their property. Treat others the way you would want to be treated. In fact, don't just be a good citizen, be a great one!

## TRY THIS!

You can be a good citizen by doing so many different things. Make a list of all the things you already do. Then make a list of what you would like to do. See how many things you can check off your list this year!

# Glossary

charity: an organization that helps people in need

citizen: a person who lives in a certain place, such as a city or state

community: a place where people live, work, and play

council: a group of people elected to make decisions

governor: a person elected to lead a state

landmark: an important place, building, or monument

law: a rule made by the government to keep order

mayor: a person elected to lead a city or town

mock election: an election for the purpose of education

pollute: to make unclean or harmful to living things

property: something that is owned

public transportation: a way of getting the public from place to place, such as by bus, subway, or train

recycle: to send materials to a place where they can be made into something new

reduce: to make or use less

reuse: to use again

role model: a person who sets a good example for others

school board: a group of people who make decisions for the local public schools

tax: money that people pay for government services

# What Did You Learn?

See how much you learned about being a good citizen. Answer *true* or *false* for each statement below. Write your answers on a separate piece of paper.

**1** A governor is the leader of a state.
True or false?

**2** Students elect school board members.
True or false?

**3** U.S. citizens elect a president every two years.
True or false?

**4** A good citizen respects people and property.
True or false?

**5** The three R's are reuse, return, and recycle.
True or false?

Answers: 1. True, 2. False (Local citizens elect school board members.) 3. False (U.S. citizens elect a president every four years.), 4. True, 5. False (The three R's are reuse, reduce, and recycle.)

# For More Information

## Books

Barraclough, Sue. *Recycling Materials.* Sea-to-Sea Publications, 2008.

Bedesky, Baron. *What is a Government?* Crabtree Publishing Company, 2009.

Hewitt, Sally. *Reduce and Reuse.* Crabtree Publishing Company, 2009.

Kalman, Bobbie. *What is a Community from A to Z?* Crabtree Publishing Company, 2000.

Kroll, Virginia. *Good Citizen Sarah.* Albert Whitman & Company, 2007.

Reynolds, Mattie. *Sharing with Others.* Red Chair Press, 2013.

Small, Mary. *Being a Good Citizen: A Book About Citizenship.* Picture Window Books, 2006.

# Web Sites

**Ben's Guide to U.S. Government**
http://bensguide.gpo.gov

**EPA: Recycle City**
http://www.epa.gov/recyclecity

**KidsHealth: Be a Volunteer**
http://kidshealth.org/kid/feeling/thought/volunteering.html

**Kids in the House**
http://kids.clerk.house.gov

**PBS Kids: Sid the Science Kid**
http://pbskids.org/sid/cleanup.html

**The Random Acts of Kindness Foundation**
http://www.randomactsofkindness.org/kindness-ideas

**Note to educators and parents:** Our editors have carefully reviewed these web sites to ensure they are suitable for children. Web sites change frequently, however, and we cannot guarantee that a site's future contents will continue to meet our high standards of quality and educational value. You may wish to preview these sites and closely supervise children whenever they access the Internet.

# Index

## **About the Author**

Rachelle Kreisman has been a children's
writer and editor for many years. She is
the author of several children's books and
hundreds of *Weekly Reader* classroom magazines.
When Rachelle is not writing, she enjoys going to
places in her community. She likes taking walks,
hiking, biking, kayaking, and doing yoga.